WALKING WITH GOD:

PRINCIPLES OF SEPARATION IN

CHRISTIAN LIFE AND SERVICE

JOHN TERRELL

Copyright © Hayes Press 2017

Published by:

HAYES PRESS Publisher, Resources & Media,

The Barn, Flaxlands

Royal Wootton Bassett

Swindon, SN4 8DY

United Kingdom

www.hayespress.org

Unless otherwise indicated, all Scripture quotations are from the Revised Version Bible (Public Domain). Scriptures marked NIV are from New International Version®, NIV® Copyright © 1973, 1978, 1984, 2011 by Biblica, Inc.™

I0201505

Table of Contents

FOREWORD

When Christians have a conviction before God that they must give expression to certain principles in divine service, the question immediately arises as to how they should relate to fellow-believers who do not share their conviction. This, in greater or lesser degree, concerns most Christians at some time during their service for the Lord. It occasions varying degrees of separation between them in service; for some more complete than for others depending on how they view the importance of the issues dividing them. Underlying the attitude of many seems to be the assumption that matters of spiritual judgment and biblical interpretation are so complex and individual that it borders on arrogance to take too firm a stand on many scriptural issues.

When churches of God separated from the Brethren movement just over 100 years ago, having had their historical roots in the Brethren movement, the very decision to take the stand they did was undergirded by the conviction that the Lord was restoring a pattern of divine service clearly set out in the New Testament; that the position they had reached was the culmination of a progressive movement of the Holy Spirit over many years. To 'keep in step with the Spirit' (Gal.5:25 NIV) seemed clearly to require a separated witness to the truths being expressed concerning the basis of church fellowship and service. The brothers and sisters concerned were well aware that they would be seen by some as another sect and so their heart-searching was deep and prolonged before they took their stand. This booklet is intended to show the positive purpose that underlies their separated witness to what they believe represents' ... the whole counsel of God' (Acts 20:27) and '... the faith which was once for all delivered to the saints' (Jude v.3).

It sets out the principles of separation as practised by the churches of God in the wider perspective of these principles throughout God's dealings with men and nations; and tries to do this in sincere humility and also with the firm purpose that the Name of the Lord of all authority will be honoured. It is in this spirit that the booklet has been written for the fuller information of new and younger disciples in the churches of God, and as an explanation of the position to interested fellow-believers. May the Lord use it to His glory.

John Terrell

SUMMARY OF CONTENT

———

E very believer on the Lord Jesus Christ should follow Him. It was of such that He said, 'They are not of the world, just as I am not of the world' (John 17:16). To be a disciple of the Lord Jesus Christ, therefore, entails separation to Him, from the world, and from wrong teaching. For the disciple, separation is directed in spiritual things towards a wholly positive end. It is primarily to the Lord. Issues relating to our personal life and to our relationships with others present themselves both in regard to the world and among fellow-believers. These need to be resolved in keeping with the Lord's command. God had a purpose for humankind when he chose Abraham who became a separated individual in both his secular and religious life. This involved weighty considerations. It involved parting from his nephew Lot who, though righteous, had gone astray. At a later date, Jacob described Joseph as 'him who was separate from his brothers' (Gen.49:26). Soon God's purposes in separated individuals developed in the separated people and nation.

Israel was redeemed from Egypt and was consecrated and separated at Sinai in commitment to obedient service to God. So a sanctuary and dwelling place for God on earth were established. National failure on Israel's part led to captivity and exile. There, personal separation to God and his laws was demonstrated by Daniel and others; and the returning 'remnant' faced sharp issues on collective separation, both secular and religious. In God's New Covenant purposes the 'Great

Commission' of Matthew 28:19,20 is all important; the making of disciples, baptism, and teaching; what Paul later called '... the whole counsel of God' (Acts 20:27). Jude v.3 distinguishes between our 'common salvation' and '... the faith that was once for all delivered unto the saints' - the full-bodied doctrine of the Lord for his New Testament people.

The practical issues involved with 'contending earnestly' for these are illustrated in Acts 15 where the 'Jerusalem Council' is recorded. Here the apostles and elders found the mind of the Lord by prayerful discussion of the Scriptures, seeking and finding the Holy Spirit's guidance which, in turn, became decrees for all the churches of God to keep (Acts 15:25,28; 16:4). This provides an important scriptural model for our day; the elderhood of God's people collectively determining the Lord's will by prayer and mutual consultation.

Churches of God need to distance themselves from wrong teaching (Acts 20:29,30; 2 Peter 2:1) and to reflect the principles of 2 Corinthians 6:14 - 7:1, 'Be not unequally yoked with unbelievers'. This passage certainly warns of the incompatibility of righteousness and unrighteousness, of light and darkness. We need to consider how far this can be safeguarded by disciples in churches of God apart from a clear separation in collective Christian service from wrong teaching and practice. The prize is His 'I will receive you' and a precious closeness of fellowship with Him in service.

Of cardinal importance to the disciple of the Lord Jesus is separation from 'the world' — from values and practices which are contrary to the teaching of the Lord and His Word. This we have in 1 John 2:15: 'Love not the world ...', and '... godliness with contentment is great gain' (1 Tim.6:6). It seems clear that early New Testament churches of God disappeared. Only after many centuries, during which individuals and companies of Christians in some countries were faithful to important scripture doctrines, did the Scriptures become freely available again. This led to progressive restoration of divine truth, and about 100 years ago churches of God were re-established. To express the truths of the House and Kingdom of God required separation from Christian denominations, and this situation is no different today. The New Testament Scriptures present a pattern of Christian unity in service which must be binding until the Lord returns.

Christian witness today should be to 'the whole counsel of God', including baptism and addition to a church of God; and continuing steadfastly in the apostles' doctrine (Acts 2:41,42). Separation is about walking with God in the light of His Word. God's purposes in separation are strongly positive in intent and bound up with the glory of His Son. We must never lose sight of this. A more detailed account of the re-emergence of churches of God is given in 'The Search for the Truth of God' (available from Hayes Press).

Some other aspects of separation in Christian life and service concern things which are 'lawful but not expedient'; handling some personal relationships as, for example, with fellow Christians once in a church of God but no longer so; how to be faithful to the Lord yet positive and helpful towards recovery; and avoiding, as far as possible, being misunderstood as harsh or uncaring while at the same time standing fast by convictions about the truth. In summing up, the basic issues of obedience, faith and love for the Lord, stand pre-eminent; and we can joyfully anticipate a heavenly future with no cause for separations.

CHAPTER ONE:
INTRODUCTION

———

'Go ye therefore, and make disciples of all the nations, baptizing them into the name of the Father and of the Son and of the Holy Spirit: teaching them to observe all things whatsoever I commanded you: and lo, I am with you alway, even unto the end of the world' (Matt.28:19,20).

The Christian rejoices to hear of new disciples being made, of hearts and lives changed to the glory of God by the gospel of Christ. He is well aware that his new brother or sister in Christ has embarked on a pilgrimage which offers the joy and peace of daily fellowship with the Lord and with fellow believers. It will also, however, present challenges in the face of the temptations of a relentless adversary. The new Christian will soon have decisions to make, some of which will call for heart searching in which the prayerful support of fellow Christians will be invaluable. Many of these decisions will concern relationships with family, friends, neighbours and colleagues.

Happy is the newborn child of God if he or she learns early that a primary concern is a frank and clear witness to the new assurance and peace received through faith in the living Saviour. Rebuffs, and even contempt, may be the response from some quarters; but this will draw the Master nearer in the comforting fellowship of His suffering. Then will come the joyful day when the Lord takes up and blesses the witness, and the happiness of usefulness in His service more than compensates for rejection and indifference. Issues will present themselves which will call for careful considerations, both in the intensely personal inner life of the spirit, and also in relationships with others. Questions will arise which need to be answered in these two main areas of Christian life. Disciples must consider their attitude to 'the world' as described in 1 John 2:15-17: 'Love not the world, neither the things that are in the world ... the world passeth away, and the lust thereof: but he that doeth the will of God abideth for ever'.

This will introduce questions about relationships with people who are not Christians and whose whole, or main, concern is with 'the world'. Then the disciple will soon also be concerned with relationships with fellow Christians. One of the earliest decisions to be faced here concerns the choice of a place of worship and Christian fellowship and service. More will be said about this in due course and about the relevance of separation which is something most Christians find themselves practising to some extent in their search for a sound pattern of service for the Lord. It is the matter of love for, and fellowship with, Him which is central. Separation, which may tend to strike a negative note in our minds, is in fact directed in spiritual things towards a wholly positive end.

It will become apparent in the pages which follow that the application of separation in various respects by God was an expression of a strongly positive purpose to exclude all that was at variance with His will and commands.

CHAPTER TWO: IN THE BEGINNING

It is helpful to go right back into the early dealings of God with men and women and briefly observe the 'what', 'when', and 'why' of those purposes of God which involved aspects of separation. This concerned some individuals who played a large part in the development of God's plan of grace for the human race. The very earliest separation God made as Creator pre-dated the creation of man and symbolized the underlying reason for all forms of separation in the affairs of God and men. This was the separation of light from darkness when 'God called the light Day, and the darkness He called Night' (Gen.1:5).

Our minds immediately turn to John 3: 19: '... the light is come into the world, and men loved the darkness rather than the light; for their works were evil'. The analogy of darkness and sin is stark, and the identification of light with gospel truth and the joy it brings, stands out in the pages of Scripture. God's question, 'Where art thou?' evoked a despairing response from Adam, 'I hid myself' (Gen.3:9,10). So the cruellest separation of all for the human race began and the supreme separator, death, began its fearful reign of terror (Rom.5:12). From that moment onward every form of separation in which God involved the human race was concerned with the conflict of sin and righteousness in one form or another. As far as men and women were concerned the central issues were faith, righteousness and obedience to the Word of the Lord. Thus very early on, Cain's self choosing and Abel's submission to the will of God about sacrifice, brought their certain result - suffering for righteousness's sake on Abel's part, and divine judgment on Cain's rebellion and disobedience.

And when the affront of human sin to divine righteousness became no longer bearable by God, the separation had to be made of Noah, '...for thee have I seen righteous before me in this generation' (Gen.7:1). Previously Enoch's separated walk with God had resulted in God taking him out of the world in a dramatic gesture of approval.

Only passing reference can be made to major aspects of separation in the early history of mankind. Repeatedly there had to be a separation of 'light' from 'darkness' in the spiritual sense; and when the time came for the unfolding of God's gracious plan for the establishment of a holy nation in this world, it must begin with a separated man. That man was, of course, Abraham. Let us observe that, in Abraham's experience, a thorough-going act of separation heralded the opening of a wholly positive purpose of God which would embrace all mankind in the grace of God when this appeared in the person of His Son, '... bringing salvation' (Tit.2:11).

Abraham - Separation and Promise

God's call to Abraham is recorded in Genesis chapter 12. From the text there we might conclude that this call was received by Abraham in Haran. However, the Holy Spirit reveals through Stephen, in Acts chapter 7, that the call came to him while he was still in Mesopotamia. This is important because of its relevance to Abraham's separation. It was out of Ur of the Chaldees in Mesopotamia (the Iraq of today) that Abraham was called to the divine purpose of fathering a great nation, receiving a great name, and being made a universal blessing (Gen.12:1-3). Ur, at that time, represented some of the highest human attainments in culture and commercial prosperity. It was regarded as a highly developed civilization, and in it Abraham would appear to have been acknowledged as a successful person by the usual worldly criteria.

Moreover, the country was devoted to the worship of moon deities, thus combining material and business wealth with frank idolatry. How far, if at all, Abraham was ever involved in the latter we cannot tell. But he recognized, by faith, that God's purpose in him could not be pursued in Ur, nor even in Haran where he remained until his father died. The land of Canaan had been presented as the objective, and in due course Abraham's separation was, geographically, complete and '... into the land of Canaan they came' (Gen.12:5). Thus God's man of destiny must know separation from both secular and religious entanglements of the world he had grown up in, and become a pilgrim for God and the spearhead of a glorious design. While Abraham was called out, what was really important was that to which he was brought. His separation was to God and His plan, again underlining that God's separations are essentially of positive intent.

When Abraham reached the land of God's promise he built an altar, indicating that the worship and service of God was central in the whole project.

In Spite of Failure

Even, however, when God separates men and women for His own great purposes, He is prepared to show long-suffering and patience when their human frailties emerge. Great man of faith that Abraham was, he faltered in the face of famine and the episode of his recourse to Egypt brought him no credit (Gen.12:10-20). His descendants had later to endure 400 years of trial and suffering there before they in turn experienced one of God's great separations in the Exodus. The material success, flocks and herds, which Abraham and Lot amassed in Egypt seemed only to occasion strife between them. This led to their separation from one another. Little wonder that Bible students have instinctively associated Egypt with the world in typology.

It is very instructive to note that Abraham's experience of separation was not only from Ur and all it represented that was alien to God's thoughts. It was also from his own nephew when Lot chose the well-watered plains of Jordan in the considerate arrangement his uncle made with him. The tent pitched by Sodom soon gave way to a city home, while Abraham greeted his heavenly visitors by the door of his tent, pilgrim to the end. Lot's efforts to make a righteous impact on Sodom were fore-doomed. Abraham, the tent dweller, became suppliant for Lot in the depraved city of Sodom. All of this contains much instruction about God's principles of separation. It is separation from the world, its materialism and its religious error. It may also have to be from others, even loved ones, who are faithful and righteous, as Lot was in considerable degree, but who make wrong decisions and move out of the mainstream of God's spiritual purposes for his own. We shall show in due course how this principle applies in our own times.

As God pursued His purposes of grace through the chequered careers of Isaac and Jacob, His patient dealings with them are recorded. Isaac's defection to Egypt mirrored his father's, and incurred similar hazards; will generations of men never learn? Jacob's entanglements with Laban after his deception of his brother Esau, brought their own sorrows. Yet the God who had separated Abraham for His own designs ultimately made Jacob, the supplanter, a prince of God at Peniel (Gen.32:22-32). He had been brought by God at an early stage of his career to Bethel (House of God) and introduced to the truth of a dwelling place for God among a consecrated people. They were almost Jacob's last words when he described Joseph as '... him that was separate from His brethren' (Gen.49:26).

Although Joseph was separate in the superiority of character he showed, yet his most precious words to his unfaithful brothers were, 'Come near to me, I pray you' (Gen.45:4). Our Lord Jesus, 'separate from sinners', is not ashamed to call redeemed and restored ones, 'His brethren' (Heb.2:11).

CHAPTER THREE: A HOLY NATION

―――――

I t has often been remarked that the last words of the book of Genesis are, '... a coffin in Egypt'. The coffin was Joseph's, but in the previous verse we have the oath he made the children of Israel swear, '... ye shall carry up my bones from hence'. Joseph was a man of sufficient perception to understand that God's designs for the children of Israel would not be fulfilled in Egypt. He shared the vision of his grandfather Abraham, '... God will surely visit you, and bring you up out of this land into the land which He sware to Abraham, to Isaac, and to Jacob' (Gen.50:24-26).

Longfellow gave us the words, 'Though the mills of God grind slowly, yet they grind exceedingly small'. Thus it was probably over 200 years after Joseph's wagons brought his father and family down to Egypt, that God began again to activate visibly the plans He had confided to Abraham, and the promises He had given him. Separated from the court of Pharaoh, after miraculous divine intervention in his infancy, Moses entered a prolonged period of preparation for leadership. During this he had to remember, and be ready to use, some of the skills learned in Pharaoh's court. Others he had to unlearn in the 'university' of the wilderness. How like the learned Pharisee of Tarsus. Paul '... conferred not with flesh and blood' when he had been '... separated ... even from my mother's womb', but, '...went away into Arabia' (Gal.1:15-17) and there he was taught by God.

Such men were prepared by God to carry forward the grand undertaking He had in view. In each case, in Old Testament and in New Testament, this involved a separated people for God's own possession.

A Coming Out

Many readers will be familiar with the development of all this in relation to the nation of Israel. From the starting point of God's holiness revealed to him at the burning bush, Moses set about, if rather reluctantly, the daunting tasks of the leadership of the exodus. God had taught him who He was: 'I AM THAT I AM' (Ex.3:14,15). It is good to pause and reflect on the holiness and eternal greatness of the God who was about to separates a people for Himself out of Egypt and to press forward with the divine counsels determined from eternity. When we come to consider how the element of separation applies in the development of the new covenant, we must never forget that the same God of infinite holiness is in command.

Staying with the story of Israel and the exodus, we recall the struggle with Pharaoh, and how the hardness of his heart so persistently obstructed God's intentions. A propensity to such hardness soon revealed itself in the liberated people themselves, and the warning from this comes down unmistakably to our day in the admonition of Hebrews 4:7: 'Harden not your hearts'. Finally Pharaoh said, 'I will let you go ... only ye shall not go very far away' (Ex.8:28). The lesson for us hardly needs to be spelled out. God's separations are according to His standards and brook no compromise with human adjustments. Again the King of Egypt tried to limit the extent of the exodus, '... go now ye that are men', and, '... only let your flocks and your herds be stayed (Ex.10:11,24).

This was not God's intention when the repeated command was brought by Moses, 'Let my people go, that they may serve me' (Ex.9:1). It was not to be Pharaoh's night, planned and executed after his views. The word was, '... this is that night of the LORD' (Ex.12:42). And so the children of Israel were brought out of Egypt by '... a mighty hand, and with an outstretched arm' (Deut.26:8), having been, as 1 Corinthians 10:2 instructs us, '... all baptized unto Moses in the cloud and in the sea'. When we come to speak of new covenant times, baptism in its symbolism of death and resurrection is an important step in the separation of the disciple of Christ for the positive objectives of service that God has for him or her.

Then, at Sinai, the challenge was presented to Israel, 'Now therefore, if ye will obey my voice indeed, and keep my covenant, then ye shall be a peculiar treasure unto me from among all peoples: for all the earth is mine: and ye shall be unto me a kingdom of priests, and an holy nation ... and all the people answered together, and said, All that the LORD hath spoken we will do' (Ex.19:5,6,8). Among Moses' last words were these, 'When the Most High gave to the nations their inheritance, when he separated the children of men, he set the bounds of the peoples according to the number of the children of Israel. For the LORD's portion is his people' (Deut.32:8,9).

A People and Their God

Thus a separated people, nation, and kingdom was established by God for the outworking of His universal counsels of grace. Soon, the heart of this divine project was the dwelling place of God among His people, foreshadowed to Jacob at Bethel. This was first expressed in the tabernacle sanctuary, and later in the temple in the land. A close parallel in spiritual terms can be shown for New Testament times. The failure of the people of Israel to realize all the high ambitions their God had for them was simply down to *disobedience*. Thus it was demonstrated that God's high aspirations for His separated people hinged on their willingness to follow through on their initial commitment of *obedience* at Sinai.

Among the grim consequences of their persistent failure was the captivity, first of Israel, then of Judah also. Balaam had been enlightened by God to declare Israel '... a people that dwell alone' — alone with their God and '... not be reckoned among the nations' (Num.23:9). Now in captivity, they were experiencing separation of a different sort, separation from God's house, the place of God's name, and the land of His promise. Separation to God and the things that He values is not a privilege to be traded for the world, secular or religious. It is true of course, there are dimensions to the matter of separation for the disciples of Christ in our day which did not present to Israel in the past, but it is highly important that we grasp the basic principles which stand out in their experience.

But God had not finished with his people in their judgement-by-captivity. The next stage of their history had its own lessons to offer on separation.

Captivity and Return

In tracing the principles which affect aspects of separation in Scripture, it is well worth while staying for a little while with this period of Israel's history. It offers significant guidance and warning at both the individual and collective levels. The resolute stand of Daniel and his noble companions, Shadrach, Meshach and Abednego, in separation from dietary defilement provides a shining example in Holy Scripture (Dan.1). This has influenced and encouraged many a young disciple of Christ. It will be very apparent when we speak of separation in our own day and age, that many complexities beset the disciple's path. It was so with Daniel and his fellows. Yet by divine guidance, through prayerful devotion, these young men found a way through a complicated maze.

'Wherewithal shall a young man cleanse his way? By taking heed thereto according to thy word' (Ps.119:9). They fixed their eyes on central and essential issues. The opportunity to avail themselves of higher education in the learning and tongue of the Chaldeans was accepted. Insofar as this enabled them the better to be useful citizens and prepare for positions of administrative responsibility, it was to be welcomed. But it also involved a crucial test of their separation as belonging to the people of God with lives regulated by the law of God. The story of their courageous stand in the matter of 'the king's meat' is well known; so is the outcome of the brave attitude of the three young men concerning Nebuchadnezzar's statue in the plains of Dura. Further promotion in their careers actually followed, but this was not the important issue. The name of the Lord had been glorified; and if that result had been achieved by the three companions being consumed in the king's furnace that would have been equally acceptable to these heroes of Israel in exile.

Separation in Restoration

It is when we come to the story of the returning remnant from Babylon that we observe the challenge of separation in a collective sense. Zerubbabel and Joshua led the first 50,000 back in faith with the benign support of Cyrus the king of Persia. He himself was operating within the over-ruling providence of God (Is.44:28). Having re-established altar services, and laid the foundation of the temple, they soon faced issues of separation from the mixed-race people of the land. The latter were aliens as far as Israel's national covenant with God was concerned. When their offer of collaboration with the returning Israelites was wisely and resolutely declined, their underlying antagonism emerged in its true colours. Soon they had contrived to cause the work of building to be suspended. It was 18 years before it re-commenced under the stimulation of the prophets Haggai and Zechariah. The stand taken in separation from the people of the land was right even although it resulted in delay in the completion of the re-building of God's house. This was ultimately accomplished but, had compromise been accepted, the result would not have achieved the Lord's will for His remnant people. The house of God of the days of Ezra and Nehemiah might never have been restored.

Subsequently compromise on the family front involving mixed marriage, also called for severe correction and separation. Earlier restraint from forming the wrong unions would have prevented the pain which followed (Ezra 10). The exact picture in our own day does not correspond in every detail but the strong principles involving separation are evident. This includes the faithful pursuit of God's positive plan for His people and their spiritual service, whatever the immediate disadvantages may seem. Let us keep in clear focus Nehemiah's prayer as he turned away from intimidating threats, and even more subtly tempting offers of collaboration. 'But now, O God, strengthen thou my hands' (Neh.6:9).

CHAPTER FOUR: THE NEW COVENANT COMMUNITY

It is time now to turn to the subject of separation in the context of New Testament teaching and example. Aspects of the subject soon emerge in the early experience of the apostles and of the churches of God which they planted and watered (1 Cor.3:6). Yet some of the fundamental principles were in evidence in the ministry of the Lord Jesus Himself. He foreshadowed the essential structure of a new holy nation, and the necessary guidance to be provided by the Holy Spirit (John 16:13). This emerges in such practical matters as the handling of church problems, as set out in Matthew 18:15-17. Time must elapse and circumstances develop in which the Holy Spirit would come and guide 'into all the truth'. This would throw into sharp relief some of the doctrinal errors of which the apostles soon had to warn churches.

Right up to the suffering of the cross, the Master's main preoccupation had been the instruction of His disciples about the reality of the crisis ahead; both His suffering and His triumph in resurrection. Once the accomplishment of these was past, the Lord engaged in a period of instruction of His own on '... the things concerning the kingdom of God' (Acts 1:3). This was in preparation for the clothing 'with power from on high' at Pentecost; the commencement of the building of 'my church'; and the establishment of the first church of God in Jerusalem (Acts 2:42). We should note, however, the foreshadowing of a separated New Testament people of God in the Lord's words as He stood on the Galilean mountain, with its view of all points of the compass: 'Go ye therefore, and make disciples of all nations, baptizing them into the name of the Father and of the Son and of the Holy Spirit: teaching them to observe all things whatsoever I commanded you: and lo, I am with you alway, even unto the end of the world' (Matt.28:19,20).

The Master envisaged a believing, baptized, obedient community of men and women. And as His apostles stepped out into the world of their day bearing such a divine remit, they can hardly have been surprised when controversy arose in matters of doctrine, and human failure supervened in the service of the churches. As in our day, sometimes these were the result of frank disobedience, as in the case of moral lapses: sometimes the outcome of honest attempts to reconcile new convictions with old in interpreting the will of the Lord.

Under Grace

One prominent issue in those early days was the apparent conflict between aspects of the Mosaic law, and the new-found liberties associated with new covenant grace. Different aspects of this conflict largely occupy two of the most important doctrinal epistles in the New Testament, namely, Romans and Galatians. The glorious summing up is, '... ye are not under law, but under grace' (Rom.6.14): yet the outworking of this presented the apostles and the churches with much heart searching. It occupied their attentions in a critical way at the Jerusalem Council of Acts 15, where Spirit-given discernment led to conclusions which were delivered to the churches as decrees.

As a result, '... the churches were strengthened in the faith, and increased in number daily' (Acts 16:5). A clear line of separation had to be determined for the new covenant community of churches of God; separation from a religious commitment which conflicted with 'whatsoever I commanded you' (Matt.28:20). Today some similarities to this can be seen in the service of disciples in churches of God who are surrounded in Christian denominations by very many devout, spiritually concerned Christian people, loyal to the person of our Lord Jesus; not to a religion which rejects that blessed Saviour as did the schools of the unbelieving scribes and Pharisees of early New Testament times. Yet it is also true that the problem which Acts 15 had to grapple with is closer to our own day in at least one respect. A major question then concerned those who did wish to acknowledge Jesus Christ as Messiah, but wished also to stay, like some of the Galatians with 'the works ... of the law' (Gal.3:1-5).

Unless they responded to the trenchant rebuke and correction of the apostle, they would make shipwreck of the faith. Many beloved children of God today seem able to misunderstand or even turn away from important New Testament teaching about their collective worship and service for the Lord, while owing splendid allegiance to their Master in other respects. The disciple in a church of God, sharing the privileges of the people of God and the kingdom of God, is challenged by this as he or she considers the matter of separation.

Early Christian Challenges

The early New Testament churches also faced other challenges to spiritual separation; challenges which also have their counterpart today. A regressive Judaism was not the only religious deviation to confront, the disciples of Christ. Emerging even in the apostolic age, and developing apace in the succeeding centuries, was a catalogue of destructive heresies. These included Gnosticism, Arianism, Pelagianism and many others. The philosophies and vain deceits (Col.2:8) associated with these, and their heretical teachings about the Person and work of Christ, are reflected in today's cults. In some ways the most far-reaching of all was the establishment of the papacy in Rome, because this soon embraced in its errors vastly greater numbers of people than all the others together. The disciple of Christ with spiritual insight based on holy Scripture should not be deceived by such error.

Furthermore, we readily acknowledge the requirement of separation from moral regression and failure, something which Paul had to command the church of God in Corinth to observe even to the point of excommunicating a particularly obtrusive offender (1 Cor.5:1,13). This matter will be touched on again in connection with the believer's separation from the world.

Other Errors in Doctrine

We should next consider the problems of subtler deviations from the faith which were threatening the service of the people of God in apostolic times. Perhaps one of the most telling passages on this is in Acts 20 where Paul calls for the elders of Ephesus and addresses them so movingly. The faithful apostle who '... shrank not from declaring unto you the whole counsel of God' is now earnestly calling on the elders to 'take heed' to themselves and to the flock of God; warning them of the 'grievous wolves' and 'men speaking ... perverse things, to draw away the disciples after them'. Whether these false teachers are to be regarded as true disciples or not, it is clear that they were in the business of seducing into error those who undoubtedly had been faithful. Although the adversary later gained an advantage in Ephesus by another all-too-familiar route - 'thou didst leave thy first love' - the apostle's exhortation about doctrine did not fall on entirely deaf ears, for in Revelation 2:2 we read, 'I know thy works ... that thou canst not bear evil men'.

In many of the churches the onslaught on the faith foreshadowed in Acts 20 must have been made successfully. This can only have been by stages in most cases, and we can but reflect on the challenge to separation which this must have presented at various times. Whether by excommunication in some cases, or perhaps by a coming out from a seriously compromised assembly in other circumstances, faithful men and women would find themselves in separated service for the Lord, as they tried to be true to the teaching of the apostles. This is relatively easy to envisage in relation to obvious heresies concerning the Person and work of Christ. But when teachings arose which deviated from the apostles' doctrine, about baptism or the breaking of bread, concerning matters of leadership and the elderhood, faithful men and women must have taken their stand and, regretfully, separated in service. When the corporate elderhood of a church of God gave way to the unscriptural appointment of a presiding bishop - what then?

Such points are made to suggest that the problems disciples in churches of God face today must have had their expression in embryo in the early New Testament churches, and presented challenges to separated service then as now. Certainly we can trace in the letters to the churches in Asia, recorded in Revelation chapters 2 and 3, the corrosive work of the adversary in matters both moral and doctrinal. Unless the disciples kept themselves separate from these evils, they risked the repudiation of their testimony by the Lord of the lampstands. At this point it is probably appropriate to examine the principles contained in 2 Corinthians 6:14-7:1.

'Come ye out ...'

'Be not unequally yoked with unbelievers: for what fellowship have righteousness and iniquity? or what communion hath light with darkness? and what concord hath Christ with Belial? or what portion hath a believer with an unbeliever? and what agreement hath a temple of God with idols? for we are a temple of the living God; even as God said, I will dwell in them, and walk in them; and I will be their God, and they shall be my people. Wherefore come ye out from among them, and be ye separate, saith the Lord, and touch no unclean thing; and I will receive you, and will be to you a Father, and ye shall be to me sons and daughters, saith the Lord Almighty. Having therefore these promises, beloved, let us cleanse ourselves from all defilement of flesh and spirit, perfecting holiness in the fear of God' (2 Cor.6:14-7:1).

It is surely very clear that Paul had vividly before him the reprehensible moral condition of the city of Corinth. When speaking of 'unbelievers' he certainly had in mind those surrounding the Corinthian saints on every hand, who were the blasphemers who violently rejected his message, those referred to in Acts chapter 18 when the apostle first came to the city. The terms 'unbelievers', 'iniquity', 'darkness', 'Belial', and 'idols' readily attach themselves to many of the citizens of Corinth. From such the separation of the disciples was obviously imperative. The apostle is deeply concerned here about the danger of moral and spiritual contamination of the disciples in the church. He uses strong language about these hazards, including in them frank idolatry and manifest iniquity. All the blessedness of the gracious fatherhood of God is in peril. Even touching is forbidden; all contact is to be studiously avoided: and the saints are urged to 'come ... out from among in active separation. The link with the warning of the apostle John, 'Love not the world' (1 John 2:15) is very evident.

Some students of the Word have asked whether the apostle had in mind a wider context for the term 'unbeliever'. It is true that the word 'apistos' used here for unbelievers, is also used whether in this form or its verbal form, by the Lord and His apostles about the unfaithfulness of some disciples. Examples are in John 20:27 about Thomas: '... be not faithless, but believing'; and Paul says to Timothy, 'If we are faithless ...' (2 Tim.2:13). While this thought may have been in Paul's mind in writing to the Corinthians, he does not elaborate on it, or speak directly of moral or doctrinal 'unfaithfulness' by believers. Nevertheless, it is a consideration worth sober reflection. Certainly, the concluding verse of this solemn passage, namely chapter 7 verse 1, speaks of cleansing from all defilement' ...of flesh and spirit, perfecting holiness in the fear of God'.

We do well to consider carefully whether this latter ambition can be achieved by disciples in Bible-based churches of God without a clear separation in corporate Christian service. This, in turn, depends on a comprehensive expression of 'the faith which was once for all delivered unto the saints' (Jude v.3). In 2 Corinthians 6:17 the great prize for coming out, and being separate to Him, is the Lord's promise, 'I will receive you'; an experience keenly appreciated by disciples in being added to a church of God and sharing the joy which David described in sublime poetry: 'Blessed is the man whom thou choosest and causeth to approach unto thee, that he may dwell in thy courts: we shall be satisfied with the goodness of thy house, the holy place of thy temple' (Ps.65:4).

The Unequal Yoke

Whether, then, we view the term 'unbelievers' as referring only to those who do not belong to the Lord by faith, or more widely as embracing Christians 'unfaithful' to the Lord in some important respect, we can usefully consider further the term 'unequal yoke'. When we think of a yoke in spiritual terms, our minds immediately revert to the Lord's own gracious invitation, 'Take my yoke upon you, and learn of me' (Matt.11:29). In that yoke we are glad to follow His lead. To be yoked with other people, however, implies a common understanding on objectives of service and labour. We think of the principle of compatibility in Deuteronomy 22:10, 'Thou shalt not plow with an ox and an ass together'; and Amos 3:3, 'Shall two walk together, except they have agreed?' A yoke of Christian service with fellow-believers who are seriously out of step with us in their understanding of the will of the Lord for corporate service, would surely be one example of the kind of inequality the apostle has in mind, even if it is not the main target of the warning being given in the passage. More, however, is said elsewhere in this book about the occasions for necessary separation in Christian service.

The issue of the 'unequal yoke' does, however, touch the secular side of the lives of disciples of Christ. One question asked in 2 Corinthians 6:14 is '... what communion hath light with darkness?' When darkness begins to creep into human dealings in the form of compromised standards of honesty, moral integrity, and honourable behaviour the Christian may face real problems in his association with others, be they unsaved people or even defaulting Christians. What Christian businessman, sensitive to the commands and moral requirements of the Master, would consider business liaison with such a person when responsibility must be shared for the outcome of common projects? At the same time, it is recognized that a wide variety of situations can arise in which it is very difficult to discriminate in these matters.

For example, two employees in a business, not involved in major financial or policy matters, may nevertheless share some responsibility in carrying out company policy. One may have fewer scruples than his Christian colleague. When is the latter in an unequal yoke? The subtleties of various situations can sometimes leave a disciple of Christ in a dilemma and in need of much prayer support. Wise counsel is called for to help him to be faithful to scriptures such as we are considering. Many have suffered serious loss rather than continue to risk compromising their moral separation. An instructed and sensitive conscience will direct, if there is honest submission of the matter to the Lord for guidance.

But does a place in a church of God and in the house of God, itself place restrictions on a disciple in the matter we are considering? Surely the important question here is how the circumstances of business and work, at any level of responsibility, affect the disciple's service for the Lord. Where work arrangements and relationships allow unhindered service in God's house, without any compromise of principles, no real problem arises. By the same token, as already indicated, anything presenting a threat to moral integrity or spiritual life, should be avoided. Without being over-ready to judge one another's conscience in sometimes complex situations, we should rather '... consider one another to provoke unto love and good works' (Heb.10:24).

CHAPTER FIVE: MORE ON DISCIPLESHIP TODAY

———

In considering 2 Corinthians 6:14 - 7:1 it was observed that the prevailing moral tone of Corinth as a city and state must have been foremost in Paul's mind as he wrote. Yet other issues were involved in the separation of which he spoke. The apostle could say to the church in Corinth that, '...ye come behind in no gift' (1 Cor.1:7). There were people of talent in the church there, yet teaching was necessary about the vast superiority of God's wisdom over '... the wisdom of men' (2:5-7). In spite of their natural abilities they were frankly told, '... ye are yet carnal' (3:3); and their tolerance of flagrant immorality in their own church, together with shameful behaviour at the Lord's table, underlined their susceptibility to the worst of the world around them (5:1; 11:21).

So, before going on to consider further issues affecting the separated, collective service of disciples in churches of God, it is necessary to stay a while on the subject of separation from the world and all that it offers contrary to the way of holiness. For let us make no mistake about one thing. The importance of separation from the world and its ways, is intimately bound up with separation to the revealed will of the Lord in Christian service. Let us not imagine that we can compromise the former without effect on the latter. The disciple in a church of God who is visibly '... fashioned according to this world' (Rom.12:2) in significant respects, will have no credible testimony in maintaining necessary separation in spiritual service. Little wonder that Paul was so distressed by the life style of some of the Corinthians while he was warning about spiritual dangers in the words, '... we have no such custom, neither the churches of God' (1 Cor.11:16). They were to be distinguished as churches of God by their doctrinal rectitude; but what price such conformity if their moral tone was so poor?

Love Not the World

1 John 2:15 stands out in the New Testament Scriptures in its direct and uncompromising demand. 'Love not the world, neither the things that are in the world. If any man love the world, the love of the Father is not in him'. The application of such a challenge to the life of the individual disciple of Christ calls for much prayerful exercise. Careful decisions will be called for in all sorts of details of life and life style. Tolerance, too, will be in order, for Christians will vary in some degree in their perceptions of different issues. Yet underlying all is the question of honest subjection to the word of the Lord, and continual prayerful dependence on divine guidance. Perhaps one of the most important things to be remembered is that attitudes and priorities call for studied commitment before details are considered.

We live in a world of 'isms', 'Ageism', 'sexism', and others have passed into our language. But the disciple of Christ must be wary of what has been called 'selfism'. That is the dominant 'ism' of our culture today, whether expressed brashly or subtly. It is the very antithesis of the gracious, yet demanding, word of Scripture, '... each counting other better than himself' (Phil.2:3). Such a spirit dismisses unsound speech and gossip from the lips of one who has the '... mind ... which was also in Christ Jesus' (Phil.2:5). Nor is it related in any way to a 'pietism' or sanctimonious self-righteousness - indeed it could not be further from this. The denial of self and the cross-bearing which Jesus spoke of to His disciples were associated with 'follow me'. The out-working of such a commitment to the Master and his cause will vary from person to person, based on the individual's true surrender of self and all his resources to Him. The rich young ruler stood no chance of successful discipleship encumbered by a material fortune. The Lord saw this unerringly. Yet the donation of Joseph's rich bounty, in the form of his new tomb for the burial of the Lord Jesus, was not only freely accepted but was actually enshrined in the ancient prophecy (Is.53:9). Joseph's valuable provision became devoted to the Lord.

'Come Follow Me'

There is no doubt that acquisitive materialism stands out among 'the things that are in the world'; and here too issues of attitude and priority are most important. While it is true that covetousness is not the prerogative of the affluent - poverty can breed a very corrosive form of covetousness - yet at all levels of material blessing it presents a temptation. Whenever is a little more not welcome? The disciple needs to beware of such a snare. Not only is it so all-pervasive in its subtle appeal but, more importantly, it is the umbrella under which all sorts of other temptations shelter. Of what sin did Nathan the prophet convict David when he had been deceptive, untruthful, adulterous, and homicidal? Only one – covetousness - in the parable of the poor man's one ewe lamb, cynically stolen by his rich neighbour (2 Sam.12:1-15).

Surrender, in whatever degree, to the acquisitive culture of the day has sad consequences for the Christian in so many important directions; and rigorous separation from it brings corresponding blessings. Among the adverse consequences are distorted priorities in the use of time; a gradual impairment of spiritual values; a competitive attitude in work or business which corrodes human relationships, and hence opportunities of witness for the Lord. The list could continue. Of course, there may often be a fine line in business between over-weaning ambition on the one hand and on the other a commendable pursuit of efficiency which is itself God-honouring. Let no man judge his brother unwisely in these things. Rather let each be very sensitive before the Lord and his Word in whatever circumstances he finds himself.

The Power Game

Closely linked to materialism is the pursuit of power and influence. A craving in this direction can develop at all levels of human relations, not only in senior business responsibilities. The antidote is a true understanding of biblical humility. Grovelling self-abasement has nothing to do with humility as taught in Scripture. Humility has been described as the quiet joyful acceptance of God's arrangement for a person's life, whether this involves a high level of leadership responsibility, or a subservient role in whatever sphere a person operates. The apostle Peter was destined for an important role in the early churches and prepared for this by a prominent place, with James and John, among the disciples. His brother Andrew might have wondered why he, out of the four, was omitted from the privileged group. Yet at every appearance in the gospel narrative Andrew operates with a quiet, unobtrusive grace which denotes true humility. That is something very beautiful in God's sight amid the grasping, self-promoting culture of the world.

What we are saying can all be summed up in the words, '... godliness with contentment is great gain' (1Tim.6:6) - and when visible, it separates unmistakably the disciple of Christ from the world around. Such an attitude of heart soon takes care of the details of personal life which are sometimes included under the title of 'worldliness'. The Christian's highest priority will not be in the world of entertainment and recreation. The latter can be afforded very limited time when the demands of true godliness are met. Care is also required in such matters as personal adornment, whether by dress, cosmetics, jewellery, or whatever. It is true that the plain teaching of 1 Peter 3:1-6 on these matters, refers particularly to Christian women. But men should not ignore their parallel, if somewhat different, expressions of personal promotion or advancement. All of these counsels on aspects of worldliness fall readily into place for disciples who 'Follow after ... the sanctification without which no man shall see the Lord' (Heb. 12:14).

The meek and quiet spirit which the apostle Peter rated so highly, is the foundation of the personal holiness which is set before the child of God as something of supreme value. It is so alien to the world and its culture of personal promotion, that it inevitably separates out the obedient disciple of Christ.

Like Him

This is all, of course, about Christ-likeness. It is about '...
reflecting as a mirror the glory of the Lord' (2 Cor.3:18); about
walking with Him in the light of His Word. This surely
underlines to us again that God's purposes, in whatever form
of separation He leads us into, is strongly positive in intent,
and bound up with the glory of the Person of His Son. This is
something we must never lose sight of as we pursue our subject
of separation.

CHAPTER SIX: A HOLY NATION TODAY

─────

E ven when the apostle Peter was writing in his first epistle about living stones '... built up a spiritual house'; about the holy and royal priesthood, a holy nation and a people for God's own possession (1 Pet.2:5,9), the adversary was busy. Reference was made in an earlier chapter to errors in Christian doctrine which developed apace even in the first century. Most of these were ultimately eclipsed by the counterfeit 'church' of Rome and its progressive acquisition of both religious and secular power in the world. By a subtle combination of secular and religious elements Satan had achieved more of his sinister purpose than purely religious heresies could ever have brought about.

Clouds and Darkness

Spiritual darkness gradually descended on the world which had been so favoured by the work and witness of the Lord's apostles and their spiritual successors. Both the doctrinal content and the structure of the fellowship of early churches of God were rapidly compromised, and the great movement created by the Spirit of God through the apostles, crumbled. A godly order of fellow elders in the churches of God, mutually dependent on the Spirit's guidance, as exemplified in Acts 15, gave way to an elaborate hierarchy of clergy, and the significance of the term 'bishop' became distorted out of New Testament recognition. Vital ordinances, the breaking of bread and baptism, became respectively the re-enactment of the Lord's atoning death in the Mass, and a rite of regeneration administered to both infants and adults. There was departure from the faith with the most far-reaching consequences.

Faithful Witnesses

The memory of multitudes of faithful men and women down the centuries must, however, never be forgotten - 'faithful unto death' in very many cases, while upholding many of the pure doctrines of the Lord in defiance of Rome's errors. This was particularly so in many parts of Europe and the Caucasus, and such faithfulness will have its ample eternal reward. As the 4th century gave way to the 5th and the 6th, evidence emerged of a gracious purpose of God to restore spiritual light amid the darkness of Rome. This is related to the text of Holy Scripture and its progressive study and translation from the original languages of Hebrew and Greek. The story is a long and thrilling one which produced spiritual heroes of the calibre of Luther, Zwingli, Calvin, Tyndale, Coverdale, Latimer, Knox, and many others. The quincentenary of the death of William Tyndale, Bible translator extraordinary, in October 1994 passed unnoticed by many, yet marked the life and work of one of God's richest gifts to the English-speaking world. And It has been through the latter that the written Word has gone out to many corners of the world, translated Into many languages.

Reforming Light

The Reformation threw open windows of opportunity which were exploited by strong spiritual leaders in many lands. In Britain the Wesleys were followed by Spurgeon and other great witnesses to the gospel, with counterparts like Moody In North America. During the 19th century men of strong character and devotion to the Word of God emerged in Britain and perceived the need for some return to the New Testament simplicity and purity of doctrine and church practice. The Brethren movement was born, initially, to give expression to the breaking of bread by disciples of Christ in uncomplicated imitation of the Lord's example. The ground of gathering for this purpose was the common life in Christ shared by all believers. However, there was failure to recognize and practice the true New Testament basis of fellowship in service, namely believers baptized and added to a church of God.

This prevented the wider Brethren movement from progressing to a more fully restored expression of God's house and kingdom in the assemblies established. It was this failure which came, in the latter part of the century, to stir many brethren and sisters to aspire to such a restoration. It became evident that there must be a separation to the truth which they perceived about united churches of God expressing the house and the kingdom of God; and *from* an association of assemblies which were unable to share their convictions. The Churches of God magazine '*Needed Truth*' was commenced to include teaching about New Testament churches of God, as well as a wide range of other Christian doctrine. The early 1890s saw the separation of many saints from 'open' assemblies to form churches of God, recognizing a united elderhood among the churches.

A Large Step

Disciples in churches of God today need to recognize how momentous and far-reaching a decision this was, taken in a reverent and honest sense of obedience to the teaching of the New Testament Scriptures. It was a major separation to honour the Word of God and the One who is called Son over His house (Heb.3:61). This is a very abbreviated summary of the emergence of churches of God a century ago, a subject which is treated in more detail in a publication of the churches of God entitled 'The Search for the Truth of God', The question arises for our own day, 'Is such a separation in service and witness still necessary?' While taking no pleasure in separation for its own sake, the conviction of the churches of God is that this separation is indeed still necessary.

We shall now pursue further the question of the relationship of disciples in the Churches of God to the larger denominational, and interdenominational, world of Christian witness.

Christian Witness Today

It is surely difficult to account for, and justify, the multi-denominational scene today. Many have longed to see a real unity of witness before an unbelieving world. By the same token most would recognize that the disunity we see today did not prevail in the early New Testament churches of God. They must ask themselves from time to time whether the New Testament Scriptures really present a pattern for Christian unity which was to be binding for all the years till Jesus returns; and why, if such exists in the divine Word, it has not seemed to them possible to sustain or revive it. It is also true, no doubt, that a great many Christians generally see no major problem about many denominations co-existing, so long as they collaborate with each other to achieve a certain semblance of unity. Many are not impressed by any need to pursue a truly comprehensive biblical unity. In fact, the loose links which exist between many Christian groupings involve varying degrees of separation from one another, based on personal or group choice, or convenience.

To share in the expression of the kingdom of God in our day surely calls for a close examination of what and who constitutes this kingdom; how it was expressed by those closest to its inauguration; what important areas of obedience to the commands of the King have to be addressed; and how the aspiring, obedient disciple should relate to others whom he sees setting aside aspects of the revealed will of the Lord as he has learned it from the Scriptures. It is true, of course, that the Old Testament saints of God confronted and yielded to the temptations of false religions practised by the nations around them. Today, however, many people, who profess a loyalty to the Lord Jesus Christ, find themselves far apart in many aspects of their activities. We are not here speaking, of course, of the activities of the cults such as Jehovah's Witnesses or Mormons, who indeed invoke the Name of Christ and the writings of the Word of God, yet so obviously depart from the most fundamental New Testament truths about the Person and Work of Christ.

The Content of Christian Witness

Let us take a little space now to reconsider what the New Testament presents as the content of Christian witness, for this must be the arbiter of our activities in testimony, and ultimately of our association with others in service. The Master's instruction in Mark 16:15,16 - 'Go ye into all the world, and preach the gospel to every creature' (AV) - must be read alongside that in Matthew 28:18-20, 'Go ye therefore, and make disciples of all the nations, baptizing them, into the name of the Father and of the Son and of the Holy Spirit: teaching them to observe all things whatsoever I commanded you: and lo, I am with you alway even unto the end of the world'. There is no conflict between these scriptures, the Matthew verses opening out the full meaning and purpose of salvation.

Many devout believers on our Lord Jesus Christ have devoted themselves in an exemplary fashion to the faithful preaching of salvation by grace through faith. Yet it is clear that the Master's purpose for those who were to be reached with the Christian message was more far-reaching and comprehensive. The making of disciples through the preaching of the gospel, the 'power of God unto, salvation', was quite inseparable in the Lord's command from '... baptizing them ... teaching them all things whatsoever I commanded you'. The earliest example of the apostles' outreach activity is given us in Acts 2:41,42 where it is abundantly clear just how lively in the minds of these servants of Christ was the commission He had left with them. They that received the word were baptized and added together as the church of God in Jerusalem, thereafter continuing steadfastly in the key spiritual exercises of the church.

The Outcome of Obedient Response

It must be stressed at this point that the apostles were keenly aware of the fundamental nature of what they were doing when the new converts were baptized and added. Later many more were added to the disciples who formed that first church of God in Jerusalem. Disciples who came thus to be in a church of God continued steadfastly in fellowship, the breaking of bread, and the prayers; these were the main spiritual exercises of a company of people gathered together on the basis of their obedience to the word of the Lord and His apostles, and recognisable as a visible community in divine service. Subsequently many more churches of God came into existence on the same basis. For we read in Acts and in the epistles of their spiritual service with the breaking of bread as a central point (Acts 20:7). Continuing to subscribe to the moral standards and doctrine of the Lord was essential for disciples' continuity as a church of God, as the letters to the churches in Revelation chapters 2 and 3 make clear.

Breaches of these standards could lead even to excommunication from a church of God (1 Cor. 5:13) though never affecting a person's standing as a member of the Body of Christ, and hence, of course, his eternal security. So we see that the preaching of the gospel for the salvation of sinners from divine judgment on sin was not divorced by the Lord from the responsibility of the preachers to baptize obedient disciples and bring them under the authority of the Lord in all things which he had commanded. The churches of God, when formed, were united in their common obedience to the one Lord, obeying the one faith, each individual having acknowledged the claims of the Master in one baptism. We do not find preachers in early apostolic times shrinking from the consequences of preaching all that the Lord had commanded them.

Witness in particular the consistency with which baptism was so soon urged upon those who had believed (see Acts 2:38; 8:12; 10:48; 18:8). The truth of this is further illustrated by a comparison of the following scriptures. Speaking of the gospel he preached, Paul declared, 'For neither did I receive it from man, nor was I taught it, but it came to me through revelation of Jesus Christ' (Gal.1:12). Regarding the breaking of bread in remembrance of the Lord Jesus, Paul wrote, 'I received of the Lord that which also I delivered unto you' (1 Cor.11:23). It was again Paul who said, 'Let the women keep silence in the churches: for it is not permitted unto them to speak' (1 Cor.14:34), and he added, 'If any man thinketh himself to be a prophet, or spiritual, let him take knowledge of the things which I write unto you, that they are the commandment of the Lord' (1 Cor.14:37).

To Paul, so mightily used by God in winning souls, the gospel came by divine revelation, and so did further truths such as the breaking of bread, and the place of women in the public service of the churches of God. He had spirit-given conviction about all these things, because the Lord had spoken about them. He, therefore, insisted on obedience to the Lord's will in such matters throughout all the churches of God (1 Cor. 7:17). It is this conscientious regard for obedience to all that the Lord had spoken which brings believers together in true divine unity, and it is the same, we believe, which brought about the separation of churches of God as recounted above.

The Interdenominational Approach

During the 20th century there has been increasing interest shown by Christian people in movements which brought together in service believers from different groups and churches. Evangelically minded believers from different denominations have co-operated for certain objectives, such as global missionary work, or large-scale gospel activity in nominally Christian countries. In examining the principles on which such co-operation is based, we are not sitting in judgment on heart motives or devotion in service. But we must approach this important subject in the light of the Word of God, and enquire whether such a basis of association in testimony to the gospel is in fact authorised by the Lord; or is it a substitute for the biblical plan for Christian witness, an expedient to meet the problem of widespread divisions among the children of God?

Interdenominational collaboration stands in pronounced contrast to the unity of apostolic times referred to earlier. It rather represents a short cut to a union of widely diverse elements by the expedient of agreeing to differ on many doctrinal issues, and limiting public witness to certain agreed objectives. For the purpose of evangelical activity, there will usually be broad agreement on such doctrines as the deity of Christ, the atonement, and the new birth. Beyond such basic gospel truths, however, little common understanding would be called for. The practice of some campaign directors and counsellors of referring converts back to the church with which they have had a previous association, even in the case of Roman Catholics, is alarming.

This is often linked to the policy of seeking the patronage of such churches. It is not surprising that many evangelicals have felt that to resort to co-operation with churches which are themselves unsound as to important truths, is not justified. They feel it will result in more confusion regarding Bible principles; that it will further blur the line between the true and 'other gospels'; that it endangers the spiritual experience of inquirers who are referred to unreliable churches.

Yet another very disturbing trend can be observed. This is the repudiation in some major denominations of an evangelical Christian approach to the Jews. Offence, we are told, should not be given to other religions, especially to the Jews who are seen as having much in common with Christians in what has been called the Judeo-Christian tradition. How, we may well wonder, would the apostle react to this, whose desire towards winning his fellow Jews for Christ was so fervent that he would have been willing to forego his own spiritual blessings for them (Rom.9:3)? Equally disturbing is the reaction of some clerics to a plea from earnest evangelical Christians that the gospel must be offered to those of all faiths in fulfilment of Christ's command to His disciples regarding 'all the world'. This too is rejected as divisive and risking offence to Muslims, Hindus, and others in our multi-cultural and multi- faith society. These matters are referred to in order to expose the depth of fundamental issues in evangelism which are separating people whose primary purpose is to work together. Could anything more clearly demonstrate the urgent need for a scriptural basis for common effort in presenting Christ to the world?

What About the Blessing?

It has often exercised the hearts of God's separated people that considerable blessing in the salvation of souls is seen to result from some aspects of interdenominational activity. If their basis of association is scripturally unsound, why do their efforts so often result in blessing? Can we find guidance in the Word to help with this difficulty? God's sovereign wisdom and mercy through the preaching of the gospel are seen in that unique and wonderful divine purpose of this age, the building of the Church which is the body of Christ (Eph.1:22,23). By divine ordination, that mighty purpose has developed through succeeding centuries; nor will God fail to gather in a single member of the body. Wherever believers have responded to the urgings of God's Spirit to bear witness to the gospel, whether in simple personal testimony, or in large scale witness, His word has been honoured and souls have been saved, in accordance with the will of God. For this we glorify God's name, sharing the joy of heaven over every sinner who repents (Luke 15:7).

But, we may ask, is the salvation of souls the only aspect of blessing? Surely not. Though its importance is vast, it should not fill the believer's spiritual vision to the exclusion of a wider and fuller divine purpose. For beyond salvation from the wrath of God, there is much spiritual blessing in the response of disciples to the complete will of the Lord, as the Master Himself testified during His own earthly experience:

'... I am come down from heaven ... to do ... the will of him that sent me' (John 6:38).

'...whosoever shall do they will of God, the same is my brother, and sister, and mother' (Mark 3:35).

'...Yea rather, blessed are they that hear the word of God and keep it' (Luke 11:28).

In a similar strain, the Holy Spirit moved John to write, 'I rejoice greatly that I have found certain of thy children walking in truth, even as we received commandment from the Father' (2 John 4). And again, 'Greater joy have I none than this, to hear of my children walking in the truth' (3 John 4). Paul longed that the disciples might be '... filled with the knowledge of his will in all spiritual wisdom and understanding' (Col.1:9). Epaphras prayed that they might, '... stand perfect and fully assured in all the will of God' (Col.4:12). This relates closely to what is written above about discipleship and the Great Commission of Matthew 28.

A High Ideal

So the interdenominational idea falls far short of the divine ideal. The limitation of testimony to the need for salvation from the penalty of sin, along with agreement to differ about other truths, tend to condition newly born-again believers to regard lightly many of the Lord's commands. They tend to regard as inevitable, and perhaps unimportant, doctrinal differences among Christians. If those through whom they have been led to Christ are at cross purposes on such subjects as baptism and church association, is it any wonder that babes in Christ fail to grow in their understanding of the will of the Lord? In this way, the prevalent confusion of thought and practice among believers tends to be perpetuated. While rejoicing that souls are saved, we cannot but deplore the sad confusion of teaching which is at once encountered by new converts. From this point of view, the blessing which God is able to grant is so much less than would be the case if believers were united uncompromisingly on the basis of God's Word. For then the blessing would extend, not only to the salvation of souls, but also in new disciples being gathered together in accordance with the one faith, to serve in churches of God as they did in apostolic times.

For the reasons set out above it is concluded that disciples in churches of God should be separate from interdenominational activity, and committed to their witness to 'the faith' and 'the whole counsel of God'.

'Forth Unto Him'

These words from Hebrews 13:13 will be familiar to readers. 'Let us therefore go forth unto him without the camp, bearing his reproach'. The term 'the camp' in Leviticus 4 was descriptive of the encampment of the nation of Israel in the wilderness. Jews would readily understand that Hebrews 13:13 applied the Old Testament teaching of Leviticus about the sin offering to their day - and ours. By the time this epistle was written 'the camp' expressed man's will rather than God's: Christ has been rejected and had suffered in the outside place. This teaching extends to all believers of this dispensation, whether Jew or Gentile. In all the arrangements of men, whether political or ecclesiastical, our Lord's authority is seriously compromised, if not largely set aside. But in the spiritual house, His authority should be absolute. He is Son over God's house. There must be complete subjection to Him, and obedience to all His commands, not only those that are acceptable to the majority. We must know separation from unscriptural associations and practices before we can be associated with Him in collective service on a fully scriptural basis.

It is to those who have responded to the exhortation, 'let us ... go forth unto him without the camp, bearing his reproach', that the further exhortation is given, 'Through him then let us offer up a sacrifice of praise to God continually, that is, the fruit of lips which make confession to his name' (Heb. 13:13,15). So we see that these closing verses of this wonderful epistle uniquely expound teaching concerning the New Testament people of God, and draw richly on the Old Testament fore-shadowing in the process. No doubt is left in our minds about the value God places on the priestly worship and service of a people for God in the dispensation of grace in which we live. It is here that we read of the believer's access to the holy place (10:19): of Christ as Great Priest over the house of God (10:21); of heavenly sanctuary service ordered by our Great High Priest (9:1-22); and of a range of precious things, better than those experienced by God's Old Testament people.

Separation, often an unpopular idea, exacts a price from the disciple, yet is not an end in itself, It is essentially a prerequisite for the carrying out of the Lord's will. The positive aspect of the separated position of God's house is beautifully expressed by David. 'LORD, I love the habitation of thy house, and the place where thy glory dwelleth' (Ps.26:8). 'One thing have I asked of the LORD, that will I seek after; that I may dwell in the house of the LORD all the days of my life, to behold the beauty of the LORD, and to inquire in his temple' (Ps.27:4). David was a man after God's heart, and he loved the place of the Name.

The revelation that God had a place on earth in which He would dwell with His people, was more precious to David than anything else. In the light of this he was able to appreciate more fully the beauty of the Lord, and as his spirit was stirred by the splendour of the divine presence, the sweet psalmist of Israel exclaimed in awe and wonder, '... the place where thy glory dwelleth'.

How much greater must be the interest and the pleasure in this subject of our blessed Master Himself, who is Son over God's house (Heb.3:6 RV Margin). Of Him it is written, '... The zeal of thine house shall eat me up' (John 2:17). When we reflect that the whole being of the Son of God is consumed with desire for the place of God's Name, how could we be indifferent to it, or regard it as a truth of lesser importance or beauty? Anything that is of special value to the Lord will, of course, be under continuous attack by the adversary. Satan hates the place of God's Name, the house of God, first revealed to Jacob, as mentioned earlier. He labours to obscure its significance in the minds of God's children. Nevertheless, the matter of collective worship and service in the way revealed in the Word, is important, and church fellowship is a vital subject. The Lord does have a pattern for that fellowship and that service, and blessed are those who find it and follow it.

CHAPTER SEVEN: SOME PRACTICAL QUESTIONS

―――

In the World

While it has been necessary, in an earlier chapter, to speak of separation from the world and, in appropriate circumstances, from fellow Christians in service, we always remember that the Lord Jesus prayed concerning his own, 'As thou didst send me into the world, even so sent I them into the world' (John 17:18), 'In the world but not of it' inevitably presents practical problems, and occasions decisions which are not always clear cut. One such area concerns matters which may be in themselves legitimate, yet in certain circumstances, should be avoided. Paul dealt with one such matter in writing to the Corinthians. The church leaders, guided by the Holy Spirit, had counselled the disciples to '... abstain from things sacrificed to idols' (Acts 15:28,29), When dealing with this matter, the apostle set out a principle which guides us in many other matters.

Lawful but Not Expedient

He declares, 'Whatsoever is sold in the shambles, eat, asking no question for conscience sake; ... but if any man say unto you, 'This has been offered in sacrifice', eat not, for his sake that shewed it, and for conscience sake'. The generalisation under which this advice is given is 'All things are lawful; but all things are not expedient. All things are lawful; but all things edify not'; and the even loftier general principle, '... do all to the glory of

God' (1 Cor.10:23,25,27,28,31). The main point is clear, that what may be legitimate in itself, may be inappropriate in circumstances where another may be stumbled or may misinterpret that action of the believer. To occasion the latter would not be to the glory of God. Whether it be in matters of food and drink, or the use of any other material substance or goods, the disciple of Christ is expected to consider his or her actions before the Lord, putting the welfare of others before personal convenience or comfort.

Mutual subjection, under the guidance of the Holy Spirit, also plays a part in many such matters. All this reminds us of the need for sensitive spiritual judgment, and respectful subjection one to another in many areas of practical life which impinge on the general principle of separation. Said Paul to the Romans, 'One man esteemeth one day above another; another esteemeth every day alike. Let each man be fully assured in his own mind' (Rom.14:5).

Another Problem of Relationships

Then there is another problem involving relationships which disciples in churches of God encounter from time to time. In the early part of his second letter to Corinth, Paul addresses an important matter concerning the brother excommunicated by the church because of his immoral behaviour, reference to which had been made in his first letter (1 Cor.5:1,13). He now turns to the much happier question of the individual's restoration. It can hardly be anything else that the apostle is referring to in 2 Corinthians 2:5-11 where he speaks of the saints confirming their love toward the brother. The implication is clear that, in

Paul's judgment, the time was ripe for the person's restoration to the church. He had experienced the severe judgment of excommunication which his sin called for, and this had obviously brought about the desired repentance and contrition.

A variety of circumstances may surround brothers or sisters when they find themselves outside a church of God in which they had once served. This can pose questions to their fellow saints about continuing contact with them, and how they can most wisely behave while they pray for restoration. A primary objective in the excommunication of a saint from a church of God is his or her recovery and restoration - another expression of the fact that separation in spiritual things has a positive goal. The hope for a change of heart, and retracing of steps, is equally applicable to the case of the saint who, for whatever reason, cuts himself off from a church by his own initiative. The erring man of 1 Corinthians 5 clearly called for extreme measures of separation by his fellow-saints - '... no, not to eat' (v.11) - while he was in the church and judgment was hanging over him.

How, we wonder, did he arrive at the position of heart and conscience which led the apostle to recommend restoration? The very fact that the saints were encouraged to confirm their love to him reveals surely that such a love was following him even in his punishment, and longing after him for recovery. Was his appreciation of this an important factor, we may ask, in drawing him back into the way? It certainly has been so in many cases of excommunicated saints, as they have later witnessed. How to express such a loving desire for the restoring work of divine grace calls for wisdom in each case. A premature level of social contact after excommunication or withdrawal could convey a lack of spiritual concern about the damage to the honour of the Lord caused by the events; or under-value the importance of a broken commitment to the Lord and His people. On the other hand, over-prolonged isolation of the erring individual could depress his spirit unduly and hinder recovery.

Clearly, the separated person's own attitude is central, with a rebellious or antagonistic spirit calling for a more severe response from brothers and sisters until a change for the better can be detected. This will not be promoted by pretending that nothing has changed from days of fellowship together in the church; nor by ungracious or hostile behaviour either. Just as the apostle had exercised spiritual judgment in the Corinthian case, so must we in the fear of the Lord, being seen to be concerned about, and praying for, a return to days of renewed fellowship together.

Sharing the Faith

Consider another sphere of the disciple's life where issues of separation may arise. Decisions may be called for about association with other Christians at school, work, college. This is rather different from the questions already dealt with about interdenominational activity. One-to-one conversation on spiritual things is the life-blood of Christian witness. When this extends to a group of people from diverse backgrounds sharing Christian fellowship in an informal setting, how should the disciple in a church of God react? Here again careful and prayerful judgment comes into play. I may be sharing in a situation with great potential for encouraging an unbelieving friend to think seriously about eternal things.

When does this become support for wrong doctrine in others, and so out of order? An example might be the strong influence in such a group of 'charismatic' Christians who wish to link salvation, or its assurance, to tongues-speaking. This may well call for dissociation from the group. The application of becoming '... all things to all men, that I may by all means save some' (1 Cor. 9:22), requires prayerful guidance from the Lord. In addition, however, the counsel of church elders, and other respected fellow saints is not to be neglected. It is often by such means that we can be assured of the Lord's direction in circumstances which might be quite complex.

Possible Misunderstanding

There is often a risk of being misunderstood in situations such as those mentioned above. Misunderstood by fellow saints, or perhaps more often by those we are in contact with at work, in education, or among neighbours. This may involve fellow Christians or unbelieving colleagues, and perhaps the pain of misunderstanding is the greater with fellow Christians. We remember Moses' experience, '...he supposed that his brethren understood how that God by his hand was giving them deliverance; but they understood not' (Acts 7:25). It is true, of course, that misunderstanding in matters involving separation can be the result of wilful antagonism to a witness to divine truth. This calls for prayerful patience, remembering that great example of natural resistance to the work of the Holy Spirit in the person of Saul of Tarsus, kicking against the goads.

Resistance to our words or actions may also, however, stem from a genuine anxiety or uncertainty in a person's mind about spiritual things, even while they are being led by the Spirit. How sensitive each of us needs to be to His promptings and directions in order to respond with grace and wisdom. For, at the end of the day, our attitudes which the Lord can act with and through, are those which most reflect the grace of Christ Himself. Especially in our contacts with fellow Christians, nothing could be more important than the exhibition of 'the meekness and gentleness of Christ'. In contending earnestly for the faith, Paul 'shrank not' from declaring the whole counsel of God. Was there a very understandable reticence on some occasions to pursue a vigorous defence of divine principles which are '... pillar and ground of the truth' (1 Tim.3:15)? A separated pathway of divine service in God's house will undoubtedly often be misunderstood as spiritual pride and intolerance. This can only be minimized by a transparent Christ-likeness in word and action.

A Watching World

We often remind one another that others are watching us as Christians. We must not assume that this is always with malign intent. Often it is not. Yet inconsistencies in our life and witness will be observed, and may give rise to misunderstanding, or worse. Examples can be found in secular matters such as public affairs or general life-style. The need to be separate from the world of politics lays an obligation on the Christian to show a real sensitivity in areas where politicians and their parties project great concern e.g. on the needs of the disadvantaged and disabled. Are we seen to respond in practical ways as we are able, in these fields without, of course, parading our good works?

While others are striving in, say, trade union circles, for benefits in which we will share, is 'godliness with contentment' evident in our lives?

In our church life and spiritual service for the Lord, is real unity of heart and soul visible to Christians from whom we feel a separation must be maintained? The objective of our separation is surely to witness to a fuller and more scriptural unity for believers. Let us ensure that this is not tarnished by internal divisions or disunity. Any tendency towards taking any pleasure or pride in being misunderstood is obviously to be deplored. We return to the imperative need to reflect our Master '... in all those lovely traits, which in His lowly, earthly days so beautiful we see'. 'Let your speech be always with grace, seasoned with salt, that ye may know how ye ought to answer each one' (Col.4:6).

IN CONCLUSION

I n concluding our subject of separation as found in scripture, we reflect again on the broad sweep of divine purpose in which the Lord's own are so privileged to have a part. Initial recollection of characters like Enoch, Noah and Abraham focussed attention on the paramount requirements of God for those He chooses to serve and glorify Him. These are faith and obedience, with a love responding to the love of a wonderful Saviour and Lord. As the plan for His apostles and their successors unfolds in the Acts and epistles, we see the emergence of a New Covenant community, a holy nation, a people for God's own possession. The One who declared, 'If ye love me, ye will keep my commandments' (John 14:15) can surely expect no less than a whole-hearted commitment in service in accordance with His Word. This, let us be assured, is the central positive objective set before us. Whatever separation He calls for towards this goal is a price which must be paid, ever remembering that the 'going forth' of Hebrews 13:13 is 'unto Him'.

There is a day approaching when those joined by divine grace to the Redeemer of Calvary will dispense with the concept of separation altogether in their mutual enjoyment of His presence. The barriers marking off the things of an ungodly world will have no further relevance and, with fellow redeemed ones, we shall know even as we have been known (1 Cor.13:12). The mists of misapprehension and misunderstanding, and failures of alignment with the Lord's full purpose, will have gone forever.

This is a prize, indeed '... the prize of the high calling of God in Christ Jesus' (Phil.3:14). With the apostle we press on towards that goal.

A STUDY GUIDE

———

This Study guide is intended to be used in conjunction with 'Walking With God' by John Terrell. It may be used either individually or by study groups. It consists of a series of questions based on the booklet which are designed to help, both in the study of the scriptures on this topic, and also in considering their practical application in our personal and assembly lives. Space is provided for some written answers, for on-

going reference. Those who use this material are encouraged to take advantage of the assistance and practical counsel that is available from overseers and other spiritually mature brethren and sisters.

Keith Dorricott

1. INTRODUCTION

1. This chapter indicates that our Christian lives are a 'pilgrimage'. That is, they are a journey through foreign territory to a desired destination. The foreign territory is referred to as 'the world'. However it wasn't always foreign; before we belonged to Christ it was our home. How does Philippians 3:20 indicate that this has now changed?

2. In John chapter 17 the Lord Jesus was praying for His own disciples. He referred in the following verses to how their relationship with the world had changed; how did He describe it in each case?

(a) Verse 11: 'these are ....'

(b) Verse 14: 'they are ....'

(c) Verse 16: 'they are ....

(d) Verse 18: 'I have sent ....

3. What did the Lord Jesus mean when He said that His disciples were not 'of the world'?

4. The same writer John, in his first epistle, elaborates somewhat on how the world is an alien environment to believers. In chapter 2, verse 16 what does he state are the three categories of things in the world? What does he say about it in verse 17?

5. What are some present-day examples of the three things mentioned in 1 John 2:16?

2. IN THE BEGINNING

1. These few examples from Genesis chapters 1 to 11 show clearly that God cannot compromise or mingle together things that are opposite from each other. For each example, indicate how the separation that occurred was necessary to accomplish the positive purpose of God:

(a) Light from Darkness (Gen.1:5)

(b) Adam and Eve from God (Gen.3:22-24)

(c) Cain from God (Gen.4:14-16)

(d) Enoch from the world (Gen.5:21-24; Heb.11:5)

(e) Noah and his family from all other people on the earth (Gen.6-9; Heb.11:7)

2. Please read 1 John 1:1 to 2:2; it is dealing with our fellowship with God the Father and His Son and with each other, and about avoiding and correcting sin in our lives. From this and any other pertinent scriptures, show how sin makes fellowship with God impossible.

3. Abraham's life consisted of a series of tests of separation. As he fulfilled each one by faith, he was led progressively closer to God and to achieving God's full purpose for him. From the following references, what were these occasions, and how did God respond to Abraham each time he was obedient?

(a) Country (Gen.12:1,4; Acts 7:4)

(b) Father's house (Gen.12:1,4)

(c) Relatives (Gen.13:7-9)

(d) Ishmael (Gen.21:8-14)

(e) Isaac (Gen.22:1,2)

4. Abraham's faith was clearly growing stronger through these experiences. Contrast the last of these tests with the first, in terms of how difficult it must have been for Abraham. Do you think he would have been able to sacrifice his son Isaac, knowing what promises depended on Isaac, if he had not previously had those other experiences?

5. Abraham's detour to Egypt with Lot had several significant consequences. If Egypt typifies the world, what were these worldly influences on both of these men, and how did they affect developments in their life?

6. How does Joseph's separation from his eleven brothers for those many years typify Christ being separate from His brethren?

7. Christ was 'separated from sinners' (Heb.7:26) and yet He mingled with them (Mat. 9:10). Explain the apparent contradiction in this, and how His example is of practical guidance to us.

3. A HOLY NATION

1. It seems that many men of God in the Bible spent long periods of time away from other people in preparation for their service for God. How did this occur with each of the following men, and how did it contribute to their being separated men of God?

  (a) Moses (from age 40 to 80 in the back side of the wilderness).

  (b) David (being pursued by King Saul).

  (c) Paul (from his conversion until Barnabas brought him to Antioch).

2. The need for us to be separated to God is part of God's on-going work of sanctification in our lives (that is, being made holy). This is an absolute necessity. Why is this, according to Leviticus 19:2 and 1 Peter 1:16?

3. What does it mean that God is 'holy'?

4. What causes us to have a desire to be more holy (e.g. Luke 5:8)?

5. In what way did God clearly distinguish the people of Israel from the people of Egypt on the night of the Passover (Ex.11:7; remember the typical significance of Egypt)?

6. How did Israel's passage through the Red Sea separate them from Egypt to God, and how does this illustrate disciples' baptism today (1 Cor.10:1,2)?

7. Israel in the wilderness were truly a people set apart, distinct from all other nations in the world. What were some of the things that made them unique (Rom.9:4,5; Num.23:9)?

8. What was the primary reason why the people of Israel were sent into captivity in Babylon? What is the parallel today?

4. CAPTIVITY AND RETURN

1. Why were Daniel and the other men just as adamant about not eating the king's food as they were about not bowing down to worship his image?

2. Were they following a regulation of the law of God, or else what motivated their stand of separation?

3. Why did Zerubbabel and Jesua decline the offer of help from their neighbours in rebuilding the temple (Ezra 4:1-5)?

4. Why was it necessary for the Jews to put away their foreign wives in Ezra 10:1-3 (see also Deut.7:1-8; 1 Kin.11:1-12).

5. THE NEW COVENANT COMMUNITY

It has been clear from the previous chapters that the theme of the complete separation of God's people to Him is pervasive throughout the Old Testament. We will now see that this continues throughout the New Testament, which is more directly applicable to us today.

1. One of the most frequently mentioned warnings to disciples in the New Testament Scriptures is about wrong teaching - that is, doctrine that is not in accord with the commandments of the Lord (Mat. 28:20), as also taught by the apostles (Acts 2:42). How is such wrong teaching described in the following scriptures?

    (a) Ephesians 4:14

    (b) 1 Timothy 1:10

    (c) Hebrews 13:9

    (d) Acts 20:30

2. How are we expected to put into practice our separation to God with respect to wrong teaching (e.g. 2 John 10,11; 2 Thess.3:14,15)?

3. What should we as disciples do when we are among others who are engaging in things that we know are contrary to the mind of the Lord (e.g. 2 Tim. 2:19-23)?

4. In the days of the early churches, a major threat to the faith (i.e. the doctrine of the Lord) was Judaism. What parallels do you think there are between this and the disregard by many believers today for being united in the faith?

5. How should saints in churches of God respond to opportunities to attend or participate in the activities of other groups of believers (such as: services of their churches; inter-denominational gospel campaigns)?

6. Paul writes, 'with freedom did Christ set us free' (Gal.5:1). Does this permit or encourage joint service with fellow-members of the Church the body of Christ?

7. When we turn aside such opportunities, how should we respond to accusations that we are elitist, legalistic or judgmental?

8. In 1 Corinthians chapter 5, what does Paul tell the church of God at Corinth to do with respect to the man who was guilty of fornication? Why were they to do this?

9. What are the dangers in associating with believers who engage in immoral practices?

10. What does scripture teach about distinctions we should make in our separation to God with respect to:

    (a) other believers themselves?

    (b) the wrong actions or conduct of other believers?

(c) non-scriptural churches or associations of other believers?

11. What are some of the more obvious heresies (wrong teachings) in Christian and religious circles today?

12. What are some of the less obvious errors, which cause division among believers today?

13. What could be the meaning of Paul's words in 2 Corinthians 6:14-18 interpreting the word unbelievers (Greek: *apistos*) as unfaithful ones, as explained in the chapter?

14. What condition, according to these verses, has God set for receiving us as His people, to walk among us?

15. What are some examples of being 'unequally yoked' (verse 14)?

16. What distinction does 1 Corinthians 5:9-13 make between associating with disciples who are under God's judgment for sin, and associating with people in the world who may be engaged in similar activities?

6. MORE ON DISCIPLESHIP TODAY

1. In our separation to God from the world (as distinct from other believers), the Scriptures are clear that we need to stay free from any involvement in the immorality and corruption that exists. What may not be so clear, however, and may present a more practical difficulty, is to what extent to withdraw from apparently legitimate activities in the world. Scripture does not provide a comprehensive list of such activities; instead it sets

out definite principles to be followed. A list of references setting out some of the principles is given below. How would these principles guide us with respect to our involvement in the following activities?

(a) Employment (e.g. organizations to work for; degree of executive responsibility; membership in unions or professional associations; career ambition; location and hours of work).

(b) Politics (e.g. voting; holding public office; signing petitions; political contributions).

(c) Law enforcement and the military (e.g. carrying arms; law suits; jury duty; conscription; conscientious objection; taking oaths).

(d) Entertainment and sports (e.g. as a consumer; as a participant).

(e) Financial gain (e.g. investments; lotteries; gambling; fund raising for the Lord's work).

(f) Charitable activity (e.g. what organizations; contributing money; volunteering time or goods).

(g) Dress (e.g. fashion; modesty; jewellery).

(h) Leisure (e.g. television; videos; radio; music; reading; club membership; drinking alcohol; movies; theatre).

(i) Education (e.g. scientific theories; restrictions on teachers regarding the Bible; extra-curricular activities).

References: Matt.5:33-37; 6:1-4; 6:19-21; 6:25-34; John 18:36; Acts 5:29; Rom.13:1-7; 14:14; 1 Cor.3:18-21; 6:1-10; 2 Cor.5:12; Gal.6:1; Eph.6:5-9; Phil.3:20; 4:19; Col.4:5; 1 Thess.5:22; 2 Thess.3:10,13; 1 Tim.2:1,2,9; 5:22; 6:6-10; Heb.13:5; 1 Pet.3:3; 1 John 4:17; 3 John 7

2. What helpful examples of the foregoing can you give from the life of Christ?

3. In each of the foregoing areas, what are possible positive actions that we can take to reinforce our separation to God?

4. How should we regard other disciples who conduct themselves differently on these matters than we do (e.g. Rom.14:10-13; Gal.6:1; 2 Thess.3:15)?

5. In what ways might we be guilty of the sin of coveting?

7. A HOLY NATION TODAY

1. In the late 1800's why was it necessary for men and women who saw the truth of the churches of God forming the house of God to leave other churches to put it into practice?

2. How important, in the overall life of a disciple of the Lord Jesus, is the need for him or her to separate themselves to God by being joined together with only His collective people?

3. The unity of believers in their service for God on the earth (as an outworking of their existing unity in Christ as members of His body) is clearly something that is of God. Should this unity be achieved:

(a) through collaboration with the many diverse gatherings of believers? or

(b) through all believers seeking to conform themselves to the faith, which is the singular truth of God?

4. Why is the preaching of the gospel today so often limited to the aspect of how men and women can have eternal salvation through faith in Christ, and omit the teaching of discipleship and obedience to the kingdom of God which was preached by the apostles?

5. How can we be true to God while 'respecting the faith' of various non-Christian religions and cults so as to avoid giving offence to them?

6. What are the reasons given in the book as to why saints in the churches of God should avoid being involved with (and attending) interdenominational gospel campaigns?

7. How does Hebrews 13:13 apply to us today?

8. Compare the attitude of (i) David and (ii) Christ towards God's house, with your own attitude towards it (e.g. Ps.26:8; 27:4; John 2:16,17).

8. SOME PRACTICAL QUESTIONS

1. Separation sometimes applies to things which, while quite acceptable in themselves, should be avoided because of their circumstances. Examples are: (i) marriage (after divorce); and sexual intercourse (outside marriage). How might this apply to such things as: preaching the gospel with others; and having fellowship with others?

2. Disciples are also told to avoid things which, while acceptable in themselves, could cause other people to be 'stumbled' (that is, to be misled because they think they are wrong) (e.g. 1 Cor.8:7-13). What are some examples of such things today?

3. How can we effectively show people that, while we are required to separate ourselves from what they are doing, we are not rejecting them personally or claiming to be superior to them?

(Some believers may find it difficult to understand why there are situations where believers are expected by God to separate themselves from other believers, since it seems to conflict with our common life in Christ, and since we are to love one another and not be divisive. Others may recognize the need for such separation, but think that it involves trying to find a middle ground which avoids both full fellowship and full separation. But our love to other believers and our need to be separate from them in certain circumstances are not contradictory; there are no inherent conflicts in God's ways for us. What we need is a fuller understanding of how these standards should be applied in practice so that we can fulfil both requirements in complete harmony.)

4. Just as with our separation from the world, so there are many practical aspects of our separation from other believers that require spiritual discernment of the scriptural principles. What guidance are we given, for example, with respect to maintaining our separation to God in the following situations?

(a) Marriage

(b) Attending other churches

(c) Associating with those put away from a church of God, or

engaging in sinful activity while still in it?

(d) Participating in informal gatherings of other believers (e.g. for prayer and Bible study)

(e) Using books, tapes, and other teaching materials produced by other believers

5. In each of the foregoing situations, what positive actions might be

undertaken in our separation to God?

6. What should our attitude be to those believers who are outside the churches of God:

(a) where they were once in a church of God?

(b) where they were never in a church of God?

7. In the garden in Eden, when Eve ate the forbidden fruit, her husband Adam was faced with a dilemma. If he remained faithful to God, he would forfeit the companionship of Eve; if he stayed with her (by also eating the fruit), he would lose his place in the garden and his fellowship with the Lord God. How does this illustrate situations that we may encounter where human relationships and loyalty seem to conflict with our obedience to and our fellowship with God?

8. Give your views on the following proposition: 'The over-riding principle of our fellowship with other believers not in the churches of God is that we might show our love for them by seeking to share with them the truth of God that has been revealed to us, not by seeking to share with them what they already have in Christ'.

9. How can we effectively reach out to other people with the gospel (in its entirety) without compromising our separation from them? (Give some examples from the lives of Christ and Paul.)

IN CONCLUSION

1. What are positive ways in which we as the people of God can (and do) show other believers and unbelievers that our faith is real and our loyalty to God is paramount in our lives, to avoid giving the impression that out faith is mostly a list of things that we can't do?

2. How can we have the courage and strength to consistently put into practice the truth of separation that we have learned?

Did you love *Walking With God: Principles of Separation in Christian Life and Service*? Then you should read *Elders and the Elderhood: In Principle and In Practice*[1] by JACK GAULT!

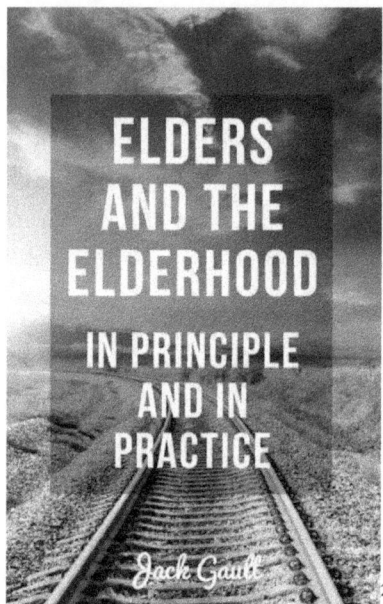

This book explores the principles of church leadership that are set out in the New Testament and how they can be applied in practice today in Churches of God.

---

1. https://books2read.com/u/3RBPXj

2. https://books2read.com/u/3RBPXj

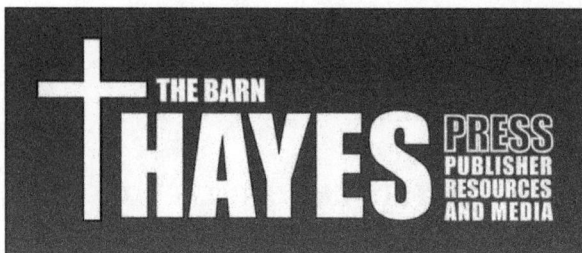

About the Publisher

Hayes Press (www.hayespress.org) is a registered charity in the United Kingdom, whose primary mission is to disseminate the Word of God, mainly through literature. It is one of the largest distributors of gospel tracts and leaflets in the United Kingdom, with over 100 titles and hundreds of thousands despatched annually. In addition to paperbacks and eBooks, Hayes Press also publishes Plus Eagles Wings, a fun and educational Bible magazine for children, and Golden Bells, a popular daily Bible reading calendar in wall or desk formats. Also available are over 100 Bibles in many different versions, shapes and sizes, Bible text posters and much more!